THE SEA MAMMAL

ALPHABET
BOOK

by

illustrated by

JERRY PALLOTTA • THOMAS LEONARD

M. is for Mac!
Keep on swimming!

Jerry Pallotta
2018

Christopher Girard, welcome to Earth.
—J.P.

For my brother, Chris, the richest man in town.
—T.L.

Text copyright © 2012 by Jerry Pallotta.
Illustrations copyright © 2012 by Thomas Leonard.
All rights reserved.

Bald Eagle Books
PO Box 52222
Boston, MA 02205
781-608-0626
www.jerrypallotta.com
www.baldeaglebooks.com

ISBN 978-0-9852032-4-5 Softcover   1 2 3 4 5 6 7 8 9 10
ISBN 978-0-9852032-5-2 Hardcover   1 2 3 4 5 6 7 8 9 10

Printed in U.S.A.
First printing, May 2012

A sea mammal lives in the ocean and needs air to breathe.

Aa

A is for ***Atlantic Spotted Dolphin***. Most dolphins are one color, usually gray. The Atlantic spotted dolphin has spots. Dolphins communicate with each other with clicks, squeaks, and whistles.

B is for ***Blue Whale***. This is not only the largest sea mammal, it is the largest animal on Earth. Its tongue weighs as much as an elephant. Blue whales are larger and heavier than any dinosaur that ever lived. When a blue whale exhales, its "blow" can reach as high as thirty feet!

The study of whales, dolphins, and porpoises is called cetology. Whales are in a group of mammals called cetaceans. There are two groups of cetaceans: baleen whales and toothed whales. Blue whales are baleen whales—they have no teeth. Blue whales get their food by filtering ocean water through their screenlike baleen.

Cc

C is for **Crabeater Seal**. What a
silly name! They don't eat crabs.
Crabeater seals eat krill by straining
seawater between their interlocking teeth.
Krill are small shrimplike sea creatures.

Seals are in a group of animals called pinnipeds, which
means "winged feet." Seals don't have arms or legs. They
have foreflippers and hindflippers.

Dd

D is for **Dugong**. A dugong is a sea cow. They have flat teeth. They are herbivores that love to munch on sea grass, seaweed, and other vegetation. Dugongs live in the tropical Pacific and Indian oceans. They have a V-shaped tail.

Dugongs have a cousin—*Manatees!* Manatees are the sea cows that live in tropical areas of the Atlantic Ocean. Manatees have a paddle-shaped tail. Manatees swim up rivers and can also live in freshwater.

Ee

E is for *Elephant Seal*. Elephant seals are the largest and heaviest of all seals. They are bigger than walruses. Baby seals are called pups, but a baby elephant seal is called a weaner.

Ff

F is for *Fin Whale*. It is the second-largest
sea mammal in the world. Fin whales are fast
and often on the move. In the whaling days, a
whaling ship had a hard time trying to catch up
with a fin whale.

Gg

G is for ***Gray Whale***. A baby whale is called a calf. Whales care for their young. Whales usually have one baby at a time. Twins are rare. The calves usually stay with their mothers for one year. Scars on gray whales are usually from killer whale or great white shark attacks.

Hh

H is for ***Humpback Whale***. Humpback whales have long side fins. They are shaped like wings. When humpbacks are cruising, they seem to be flying through the ocean.

This humpback whale is about to breach. When a whale jumps out of the water it is called breaching. Usually there is a loud splash!

I is for *Ice Bear*. Ice bear is another name for polar bear. A polar bear is a sea mammal. They live on the sea—the frozen Arctic Sea. Their paws are slightly webbed, and are wide like paddles. They are excellent swimmers. Polar bears love to eat seals and sometimes walruses.

Ice bears and arctic foxes have been known to chum around together. The bear eats the blubber and leaves some of the meat for his buddy the fox.

Ii

Jj

J is for ***Juan Fernandez Fur Seal***. These small seals live on the Juan Fernandez Islands off the coast of Chile. They were once heavily hunted for their beautiful fur. Dolphins and whales do not have external ears, but seals do. How are you like a seal? Seals have five fingers and five toes inside those webbed flippers.

Kk

K is for *Killer Whale*. Killer whales are also called orcas. Orcas are the largest of all dolphins. They are easy to recognize because they are white and black. The male has the tallest dorsal fin of any sea creature.

Ll

L is for ***Leopard Seal***. Leopard seals live in Antarctica. Leopard seals have powerful jaws. Leopard is a good name for these toothy predators. They eat fish and shellfish but prefer a warm-blooded meal. Watch out, penguins! Sea leopards would love to eat you.

Mm

M is for *Melonhead.* Beluga whales are sometimes called melonheads because of their bulb-like heads, which are shaped like melons. Beluga whales make so many different sounds and songs that they are also known as sea canaries.

Nn

N is for ***Nutria***. Wait! A nutria is a South American river rodent, which is not a sea mammal. No "rats" allowed in this book! Let's see if we can find a sea mammal that begins with the letter N. You might find one later in the book.

N could have been for New Zealand fur seal.

Oo

O is for *Otter*. River otters live in freshwater lakes, ponds, and rivers. They are aquatic animals, not sea mammals. Baby otters are called kits.

And then there are **sea otters**. Sea otters are one of the cutest creatures in the ocean. People love to watch them. They have the thickest fur of any mammal—almost a million hairs per square inch. Sea otters are known for using a rock as a tool, floating on their backs, and smashing crabs and clams to eat. They eat starfish, too!

Pp

P is for **Pilot Whale**. Pilot whales are usually seen in huge numbers. A group of fish is called a school. A group of whales is called a pod. Pilot whales travel in huge pods. When pilot whales ground themselves in large numbers, it is called a mass stranding. No one knows why they do it.

Qq

Q is for *Question.* We could not find a sea mammal that begins with *Q*. So, we'll ask a question. What is the difference between dolphins and porpoises? Dolphins are larger and porpoises are smaller. Dolphins have a pointed head. Porpoises have a rounded head. Dolphins have taller, curved dorsal fins. Porpoises have short dorsal fins.

Wait, we found a *Q!*
A narwhal is called a *qilalugaq* in an Inuit language.

R is for ***Risso's Dolphin***. This dolphin is a light color and is covered with scrape marks. When it sticks its head out of the water to look around, it is called spyhopping. When dolphins turn around and around, it is called spinning. Maybe someday you will see a spinning, spyhopping dolphin.

Ss

S is for ***Sperm Whale.*** These whales look like a giant square head with a tail. Sperm whales are the largest toothed whales. They are unusual because they have teeth, but only on the lower jaw. Sperm whales can stay underwater for longer than an hour. They can dive a mile deep looking for their favorite food—giant squid.

T is for *Tucuxi.* These small South American dolphins live around the Amazon River. Tucuxi are comfortable swimming in three different types of water:

- Coastal oceans, which are saltwater.

- Rivers, which are freshwater.

- Estuaries, which are brackish water. Brackish water is part salt and part freshwater. An estuary is where an ocean meets a river.

No sea creature likes polluted water.

Tt

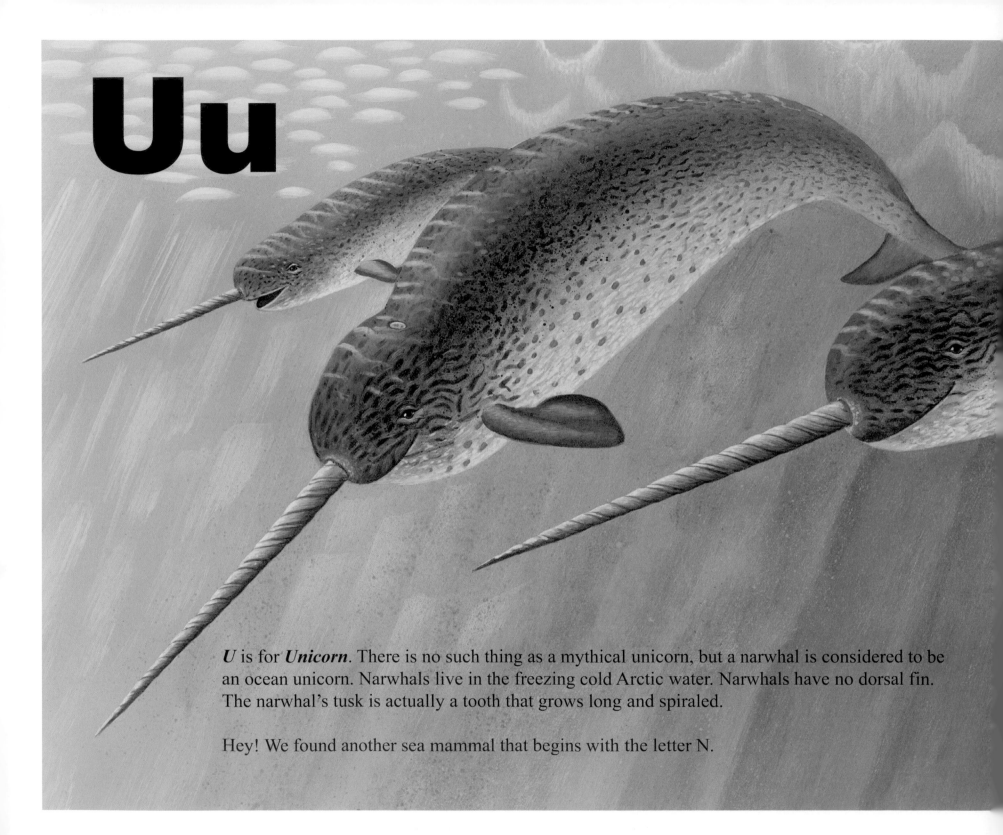

Uu

U is for ***Unicorn***. There is no such thing as a mythical unicorn, but a narwhal is considered to be an ocean unicorn. Narwhals live in the freezing cold Arctic water. Narwhals have no dorsal fin. The narwhal's tusk is actually a tooth that grows long and spiraled.

Hey! We found another sea mammal that begins with the letter N.

Vv

V is for *Vaquita*. This small porpoise is rare. It only lives in the northern area of the Gulf of California. It is also called a cochita, a gulf porpoise, and a Gulf of California porpoise. The word *vaquita* means "little cow."

W is for **Walrus.** *W* could also be for their thick whiskers. Walrus have two tusks, which they use as tools. Tusks act like ice picks to pull walrus up on ice floes. They can be used for protection and to help dig out mussels and clams, their favorite foods.

We can't find a sea mammal that begins with **X**.

We looked in the library. We searched the internet, libraries, bookstores, and aquariums. We looked everywhere, but couldn't find one that begins with the letter X.

We asked a teacher, a scientist, and a marine biologist. We even asked my mom. We could not find an X.

The closest we came was ***Arnoux's Beaked Whale***. It is a rare whale that is hardly ever seen. It swims in the oceans near the South Pole.

Yy

Y is for ***Yangtze River Dolphin***. It is also called a Chinese dolphin, or a baiji. Where are you? Where did you go? It is a sad story. Recent explorations on China's Yangtze and Qintangjiang rivers did not find even one of these small freshwater dolphins. Dams, pollution, overfishing, and boat propellers may have led to their extinction.

Zz

Z is for *Ziphius*. People call it a goose-beaked
whale or Cuvier's beaked whale. Scientists call it
Ziphius. Beaked whales are rare and mysterious.
No one really knows much about them. The Ziphius
and other beaked whales avoid people whenever they can.

Some humans love to go scuba diving, snorkeling, fishing, lobstering, shrimping, crabbing, clamming, surfing, rowing, kayaking, sailing, and boating. Maybe they should be considered sea mammals, too!